YOUR COMPLETE PISCES 2025 PERSONAL HOROSCOPE

Monthly Astrological Prediction Forecast Readings of Every Zodiac Astrology Sun Star Signs- Love, Romance, Money, Finances, Career, Health, Travel, Spirituality.

Iris Quinn

Alpha Zuriel Publishing

Your Complete Pisces 2025 Personal Horoscope/ Iris Quinn. -- 1st ed.

"Astrology is a language. If you understand this language, the sky speaks to you."
— IRIS QUINN

CONTENTS

PISCES PROFILE

General Characteristics

- **Element:** Water
- **Quality:** Mutable
- **Ruler:** Neptune
- **Symbol:** The Fish
- **Dates:** February 19 - March 20

Personality Traits

- **Compassionate:** Deeply empathetic and caring.
- **Intuitive:** Strong sense of intuition and understanding.
- **Artistic:** Creative and imaginative, often drawn to the arts.
- **Sensitive:** Highly attuned to their surroundings and emotions.
- **Adaptable:** Flexible and able to go with the flow.

- **Selfless:** Often putting others' needs before their own.
- **Dreamy:** Prone to daydreaming and imaginative thinking.
- **Idealistic:** Holds high ideals and aspirations.
- **Romantic:** Deeply loving and affectionate.
- **Escapist:** Can retreat into their own world when overwhelmed.

Strengths

- **Empathy:** Ability to understand and share the feelings of others.
- **Creativity:** Produces unique and imaginative ideas.
- **Generosity:** Willingness to give without expecting anything in return.
- **Adaptability:** Adjusts easily to new circumstances and environments.
- **Intuition:** Reads situations and people accurately.

Weaknesses

- **Over-sensitivity:** Can be easily hurt by criticism or harsh realities.
- **Indecisiveness:** Struggles to make firm decisions.
- **Escapism:** Tendency to avoid problems rather than confront them.

- **Idealism:** Can be overly idealistic, sometimes losing touch with reality.
- **Self-pity:** Can fall into bouts of feeling sorry for themselves.

Planets and Their Influences

- **Career Planet:** Jupiter – Expands professional opportunities and encourages growth.
- **Love Planet:** Venus – Influences love, relationships, and artistic inclinations.
- **Money Planet:** Venus – Also rules financial matters and a love for luxury.
- **Planet of Fun, Entertainment, Creativity, and Speculations:** Neptune – Enhances creativity and imagination.
- **Planet of Health and Work:** Mercury – Governs communication and daily routines.
- **Planet of Home and Family Life:** Moon – Governs emotions and domestic affairs.
- **Planet of Spirituality:** Neptune – Represents dreams and intuition.
- **Planet of Travel, Education, Religion, and Philosophy:** Jupiter – Governs expansion and learning.

Compatibility

- **Signs of Greatest Overall Compatibility:** Cancer, Scorpio

- **Signs of Greatest Overall Incompatibility:** Gemini, Sagittarius
- **Sign Most Supportive for Career Advancement:** Taurus
- **Sign Most Supportive for Emotional Well-being:** Cancer
- **Sign Most Supportive Financially:** Capricorn
- **Sign Best for Marriage and/or Partnerships:** Virgo
- **Sign Most Supportive for Creative Projects:** Leo
- **Best Sign to Have Fun With:** Sagittarius
- **Signs Most Supportive in Spiritual Matters:** Pisces
- **Best Day of the Week:** Thursday

Additional Details

- **Colors:** Sea Green, Lavender
- **Gem:** Amethyst
- **Scent:** Jasmine, Sandalwood
- **Birthstone:** Amethyst
- **Quality:** Mutable (adaptable and flexible)

PERSONALITY OF PISCES

Pisces, governed by Neptune, is a zodiac sign imbued with profound emotional depth and sensitivity. Individuals born under this sign are often characterized by their compassionate and empathetic nature, which enables them to connect deeply with others. This connection is not merely superficial; Pisces genuinely feels the emotions of those around them, often taking on their joys and sorrows as if they were their own. This heightened empathy makes Pisces exceptional friends and confidants, always ready to offer a listening ear or a comforting presence.

Creativity and imagination are hallmarks of the Pisces personality. They possess an innate ability to see the world through a lens of wonder and fantasy, often finding beauty and inspiration in places others might overlook. This creative flair manifests in various forms, from art and music to writing and dance. Pisces individuals are often drawn to the arts, where they can express their rich inner lives and convey the depth of their emotions.

One of the most endearing qualities of Pisces is their selflessness. They are naturally inclined to help others, often putting the needs of friends, family, and even strangers before their own. This altruistic nature can sometimes lead to them being taken advantage of, as they may struggle to set boundaries and say no. However, their generosity and kindness are unwavering, making them beloved by many.

Despite their gentle and nurturing demeanor, Pisces can be incredibly resilient. They possess an inner strength that allows them to endure hardships and bounce back from adversity. This resilience is often fueled by their ability to escape into their imaginative worlds, where they can find solace and recharge their emotional batteries. Their symbol, the two fish swimming in opposite directions, aptly represents their dual nature – a constant balance between reality and fantasy.

However, this tendency to escape can also be a double-edged sword. Pisces may sometimes retreat too far into their dream worlds, avoiding the harsh realities of life. This escapism can manifest in various ways, such as daydreaming, indulging in creative pursuits, or even turning to substances to numb their sensitivities. It's crucial for Pisces to find healthy outlets for their emotions and to stay grounded in the real world.

Pisces' intuitive nature is another defining trait. They have a remarkable ability to sense things beyond the surface, often picking up on the unspoken feelings and thoughts of those around them. This intuition makes them insightful and wise, often providing valuable perspectives in personal and professional situations. However, their reliance on intuition can sometimes lead them to be overly trusting, making them vulnerable to deceit or disappointment.

In relationships, Pisces are devoted and loving partners. They crave deep, soulful connections and are willing to go to great lengths to maintain harmony and happiness in their relationships. Their romantic nature means they often idealize their partners, which can sometimes lead to unrealistic expectations. Nevertheless, their love is pure and genuine, and they are capable of great sacrifices for the ones they care about.

In summary, Pisces is a sign that embodies compassion, creativity, and intuition. Their deep emotional reservoirs and empathetic nature make them unique and cherished individuals. While their tendency to escape reality can pose challenges, their resilience and boundless imagination ensure they navigate life's complexities with grace and heart.

WEAKNESSES OF PISCES

Pisces, while possessing many admirable qualities, also has its share of weaknesses that can present challenges in various aspects of life. One of the most prominent weaknesses of Pisces is their tendency to be overly sensitive. Their heightened empathy and deep emotional connection to others often make them vulnerable to getting hurt easily. They absorb the emotions and energies around them, which can lead to emotional overload and difficulty in maintaining their own emotional stability. This sensitivity, while it makes them compassionate, can also cause them to retreat from situations that seem too overwhelming.

Another weakness is their tendency to escape from reality. Pisces often find solace in their rich inner worlds and vivid imaginations. While this can be a source of creativity, it can also become a means of avoiding real-life challenges and responsibilities. When faced with difficulties, Pisces might choose to retreat into their fantasies or engage in escapist behaviors such as excessive daydreaming, binge-watching TV, or even substance abuse. This avoidance can prevent them from addressing issues head-on,

8

leading to unresolved problems and a lack of progress in their personal or professional lives.

Pisces can also struggle with indecisiveness. Their empathetic nature makes them considerate of multiple perspectives, which can hinder their ability to make firm decisions. They may find themselves torn between different choices, wanting to please everyone and avoid conflict. This indecision can lead to missed opportunities and a sense of stagnation. Moreover, their desire to keep the peace and avoid confrontation can sometimes result in passive-aggressive behavior or resentment, as they might suppress their true feelings to avoid upsetting others.

Additionally, Pisces can be overly idealistic. They often see the world through rose-colored glasses, which can lead to unrealistic expectations. In relationships, this idealism might cause them to overlook red flags or stay in unhealthy situations, hoping for the best. Their partners may not always live up to their high ideals, leading to disappointment and disillusionment. This idealism extends to their personal goals as well, where they may set aspirations that are difficult to achieve, resulting in feelings of failure and frustration.

Another challenge for Pisces is their tendency to be overly trusting. Their innate belief in the goodness of others can make them naive and susceptible to manipulation or deceit. They may give too much of themselves, expecting the same level of honesty and integrity in return, which isn't always the case. This trust can be exploited by those with less honorable intentions, leaving Pisces feeling betrayed and disheartened.

Pisces can also have difficulty setting boundaries. Their selfless nature often leads them to put others' needs before their own, sometimes to their detriment. They may find it challenging to say no, fearing they will disappoint or upset others. This can result in them taking on too much, leading to burnout and neglect of their own needs. Learning to set healthy boundaries and prioritize self-care is crucial for their well-being.

Lastly, Pisces might struggle with a lack of self-confidence. Despite their many talents and intuitive abilities, they can be plagued by self-doubt and insecurity. They may undervalue their contributions and abilities, seeking validation from external sources rather than trusting in their own worth. This lack of confidence can hold them back from pursuing their dreams and fully realizing their potential.

In summary, while Pisces possess many wonderful qualities, their weaknesses include sensitivity, escapism, indecisiveness, idealism, over-trusting nature, difficulty with boundaries, and a lack of self-confidence. These traits can pose challenges, but with awareness and effort, Pisces can work towards overcoming these weaknesses and leading a more balanced and fulfilling life.

RELATIONSHIP COMPATIBILITY WITH PISCES

Based only on their Sun signs, this is how Pisces interacts with others. These are the compatibility interpretations for all 12 potential Pisces combinations. This is a limited and insufficient method of determining compatibility.

However, Sun-sign compatibility remains the foundation for overall harmony in a relationship.

The general rule is that yin and yang do not get along. Yin complements yin, and yang complements yang. While yin and yang partnerships can be successful, they require more effort. Earth and water zodiac signs are both Yin. Yang is represented by the fire and air zodiac signs.

Pisces with Yang Signs (Fire and Air)

Pisces and Aries (Yin with Yang):

Pisces and Aries can have a challenging yet potentially rewarding relationship. Aries' boldness and direct approach can sometimes overwhelm Pisces' sensitive nature. However, Aries' decisiveness can help Pisces gain confidence and assertiveness. The key to making this relationship work lies in understanding and respecting each other's differences. Aries should practice patience and gentleness, while Pisces needs to be open to stepping out of their comfort zone. When balanced, Aries can bring excitement to Pisces' life, and Pisces can offer emotional depth and empathy to Aries.

Pisces and Leo (Yin with Yang):

Pisces and Leo form an intriguing partnership, blending Leo's charisma and leadership with Pisces' creativity and empathy. Leo's confidence can inspire Pisces, while Pisces' sensitivity can teach Leo about compassion and emotional connection. However, Leo's need for attention and Pisces' tendency to withdraw can lead to misunderstandings. To foster harmony, Leo must be mindful of Pisces' need for emotional support, and Pisces should appreciate Leo's enthusiasm and passion. Mutual admiration and understanding are essential to creating a balanced and fulfilling relationship.

Pisces and Sagittarius (Yin with Yang):

Pisces and Sagittarius can experience a relationship filled with adventure and philosophical exploration. Sagittarius' optimism and love for freedom can invigorate Pisces, while Pisces' introspective nature can offer depth to Sagittarius' experiences. However, Sagittarius' bluntness can sometimes hurt Pisces' feelings, and Pisces' need for emotional security might clash with Sagittarius' desire for independence. For this relationship to thrive, Sagittarius needs to be considerate of Pisces' sensitivities, and Pisces should embrace Sagittarius' adventurous spirit. Open communication and mutual respect are vital for maintaining harmony.

Pisces and Gemini (Yin with Yang):

Pisces and Gemini create a dynamic and intellectually stimulating partnership. Gemini's curiosity and adaptability complement Pisces' imagination and emotional depth. They enjoy exploring new ideas and experiences together, keeping their relationship lively. However, Gemini's inconsistency and Pisces' emotional needs can sometimes cause friction. Gemini should be sensitive to Pisces' feelings, and Pisces should appreciate Gemini's need for variety and mental stimulation. Finding a balance between emotional connection and intellectual engagement is crucial for a harmonious relationship.

Pisces and Libra (Yin with Yang):

Pisces and Libra share a mutual appreciation for beauty, art, and harmony. Libra's charm and diplomatic nature align well with Pisces' compassion and creativity. They can build a relationship based on mutual admiration and shared interests. However, Libra's indecisiveness and Pisces' tendency to escape reality can lead to challenges. Libra should support Pisces' emotional needs, and Pisces should value Libra's need for balance and harmony. Effective communication and a shared commitment to maintaining harmony are essential for a successful relationship.

Pisces and Aquarius (Yin with Yang):

Pisces and Aquarius have a relationship marked by innovation and emotional depth. Aquarius' visionary ideas and Pisces' intuitive nature can create a unique and inspiring partnership. However, Aquarius' detachment and Pisces' emotional intensity can sometimes clash. Aquarius should be mindful of Pisces' need for emotional connection, and Pisces should appreciate Aquarius' intellectual independence. Balancing emotional intimacy with intellectual stimulation is key to making this relationship work.

Pisces with Yin Signs (Earth and Water)

Pisces and Taurus (Yin with Yin):

Pisces and Taurus form a naturally harmonious and supportive relationship. Taurus' practicality and stability provide a solid foundation for Pisces' dreams and emotional needs. In return, Pisces offers Taurus emotional depth and creativity. Both signs value security and comfort, creating a nurturing environment. However, Taurus' stubbornness and Pisces' tendency to escape reality can pose challenges. Taurus should be patient with Pisces' emotional fluctuations, and Pisces should appreciate Taurus' steadfastness. Mutual support and understanding are crucial for a balanced and fulfilling partnership.

Pisces and Virgo (Yin with Yin):

Pisces and Virgo create a complementary relationship, blending Virgo's analytical nature with Pisces' intuition and empathy. Virgo's practicality can ground Pisces' dreams, while Pisces' emotional insight can soften Virgo's critical tendencies. However, Virgo's need for order and Pisces' tendency towards chaos can lead to conflicts. Virgo should be patient and compassionate with Pisces, and Pisces should appreciate Virgo's efforts to create structure and stability. Communication and mutual appreciation are essential for maintaining harmony in this partnership.

Pisces and Capricorn (Yin with Yin):

Pisces and Capricorn form a balanced and supportive relationship, combining Capricorn's ambition and discipline with Pisces' creativity and empathy. Capricorn's practicality provides a strong foundation for Pisces' dreams, while Pisces' emotional depth can inspire Capricorn. However, Capricorn's focus on goals and Pisces' emotional needs can sometimes clash. Capricorn should be attentive to Pisces' sensitivities, and Pisces should respect Capricorn's dedication and hard work. Mutual respect and understanding are key to creating a fulfilling and stable relationship.

Pisces and Cancer (Yin with Yin):

Pisces and Cancer share a deeply emotional and intuitive connection. Both signs value emotional security and nurturing, creating a supportive and caring environment. Cancer's protectiveness and Pisces' empathy form a harmonious bond. However, their shared sensitivity can sometimes lead to emotional turbulence. Cancer should provide stability for Pisces, and Pisces should offer emotional support to Cancer. Maintaining open communication and emotional honesty is vital for a balanced and loving partnership.

Pisces and Scorpio (Yin with Yin):

Pisces and Scorpio have an intense and transformative relationship. Scorpio's passion and depth complement Pisces' empathy and intuition, creating a profound emotional connection. Both signs value loyalty and emotional intimacy, fostering a strong bond. However, Scorpio's intensity and Pisces' sensitivity can lead to power struggles. Scorpio should be gentle with Pisces' feelings, and Pisces should appreciate Scorpio's loyalty and depth. Mutual trust and respect are essential for maintaining a passionate and fulfilling relationship.

Pisces and Pisces (Yin with Yin):

When two Pisces come together, their relationship is marked by deep emotional and intuitive understanding. They share a profound connection, valuing empathy, creativity, and compassion. However, their mutual tendency to escape reality can lead to challenges in facing practical matters. Both Pisces should support each other in staying grounded while nurturing their shared dreams. Open communication and a commitment to balancing their emotional and practical needs are crucial for a harmonious and fulfilling partnership.

In conclusion, Pisces' compatibility with other sun signs varies widely based on the yin and yang theory. Water and earth signs generally complement Pisces' emotional and intuitive nature, leading to nurturing and harmonious relationships. Fire and air signs, while presenting more challenges, can provide excitement and intellectual stimulation, requiring more effort to balance their differences. With mutual respect, understanding, and a willingness to learn from each other, Pisces can form successful and fulfilling partnerships with any sign.

LOVE AND PASSION

Pisces, the dreamer of the zodiac, embodies a unique blend of love and passion that is deeply intertwined with their emotional and intuitive nature. Governed by Neptune, the planet of dreams and spirituality, Pisces individuals are known for their profound capacity to love selflessly and unconditionally. Their approach to love is deeply romantic and often idealistic, as they seek a soul connection that transcends the mundane aspects of life.

Pisces' love is characterized by a deep emotional connection. They yearn for a bond that goes beyond physical attraction, seeking to merge their souls with their partner's in a way that feels almost mystical. This sign has an innate ability to sense their partner's needs and emotions, often understanding them better than they understand themselves. This heightened sensitivity allows Pisces to offer unparalleled emotional support and compassion, making their love feel like a safe haven for their partner.

In passion, Pisces is incredibly imaginative and intuitive. They are not afraid to explore the depths of their emotions and desires, bringing a level of intensity and creativity to their romantic encounters. Their passion is fluid and adaptable, capable of shifting to meet the needs and desires of their partner. This flexibility makes them incredibly attentive lovers who are always eager to ensure that their partner feels cherished and fulfilled.

However, Pisces' idealistic view of love can sometimes lead them into turbulent waters. They may fall into the trap of seeing their partner through rose-colored glasses, overlooking flaws and potential issues. This tendency to idealize love can make them vulnerable to disappointment when reality does not meet their lofty expectations. Despite this, their resilient spirit and capacity for forgiveness allow them to navigate these challenges with grace.

Pisces' love is also marked by a deep sense of empathy and selflessness. They often put their partner's needs above their own, striving to create a harmonious and nurturing relationship. This can sometimes lead to issues with boundaries, as Pisces might give too much of themselves, leading to emotional exhaustion. It is crucial for them to find a balance between giving and receiving in their relationships to maintain their emotional well-being.

In relationships, Pisces thrives on emotional and spiritual connection. They seek a partner who can understand their complex inner world and appreciate their sensitivity and creativity. A relationship with a Pisces is often marked by profound moments of emotional bonding, shared dreams, and a sense of mutual understanding that feels almost otherworldly. Their love is nurturing and healing, providing a sanctuary for their partner's soul.

Pisces' passion extends beyond the bedroom, infusing their entire relationship with a sense of magic and wonder. They are often drawn to artistic and creative pursuits, and they love sharing these experiences with their partner. Whether it's through music, art, or simply daydreaming together, Pisces brings a touch of enchantment to their romantic life.

Overall, love and passion for Pisces are deeply emotional and spiritually enriching experiences. They are devoted and empathetic partners who seek to create a bond that transcends the ordinary. Their ability to connect on a soulful level makes their love feel timeless and profoundly fulfilling, offering a unique and deeply moving experience for those who are fortunate enough to be loved by a Pisces.

MARRIAGE

Marriage for Pisces is a deeply emotional and spiritual union that transcends the mere physical connection. Governed by Neptune, Pisces individuals bring a sense of ethereal beauty and profound sensitivity to their marital relationships. They are dreamers and romantics at heart, seeking a partner with whom they can share their deepest emotions and spiritual insights. To keep a Pisces happy in marriage, it is crucial to understand their need for emotional connection, empathy, and a nurturing environment where their dreams and ideals are respected and cherished.

Pisces men in marriage are gentle, compassionate, and incredibly devoted. They possess an innate ability to understand their partner's needs and desires, often putting their loved ones before themselves. Their intuitive nature allows them to connect on a deep emotional level, creating a sense of security and unconditional love. However, Pisces men can sometimes struggle with setting boundaries and may become overwhelmed by their partner's needs if they neglect their own well-being. To maintain a harmonious marriage, it is important for their partners to offer them the same level of support and understanding, encouraging them to express their own feelings and aspirations.

Pisces women bring a unique blend of empathy, creativity, and nurturing energy to their marriages. They are often seen as the emotional anchors in their relationships, providing a safe and comforting space for their partners to express themselves. Pisces women are deeply intuitive and often possess a sixth sense when it comes to their partner's emotions. This sensitivity, while a strength, can also be a source of vulnerability if they feel unappreciated or misunderstood. To keep a Pisces woman happy in marriage, it is essential to create an environment of mutual respect, open communication, and shared dreams. Encouraging her creative pursuits and spiritual interests can also strengthen the bond and bring more joy into the relationship.

The secret to making a marriage with a Pisces work lies in fostering an environment of emotional openness and spiritual connection. Pisces thrives in relationships where they feel understood and valued for their unique perspectives and sensitivities. Creating rituals of togetherness, such as shared meditations, artistic collaborations, or simply spending time in nature, can help deepen the bond and keep the relationship vibrant. It is also important to maintain a balance between giving and receiving, ensuring that both partners feel equally supported and cherished.

For Pisces, a fulfilling marriage is one where their dreams and ideals are nurtured, and their emotional depths are met with compassion and understanding. They seek a partner who can journey with them through the highs and lows of life, offering a hand to hold and a heart to understand. By valuing their intuitive insights, encouraging their creative expressions, and being present in both joyous and challenging times, one can build a marriage with Pisces that is not only enduring but also deeply enriching on an emotional and spiritual level.

Pisces are known for their ability to love selflessly and unconditionally, often seeing the best in their partners even when others may not. This idealistic view of love can be both a strength and a challenge. While it allows them to create a deeply nurturing and forgiving environment, it can also lead to disappointment if their expectations are not met. Therefore, maintaining realistic expectations and engaging in honest and compassionate communication is crucial for the longevity of the marriage.

In essence, marrying a Pisces means embarking on a journey filled with emotional depth, spiritual growth, and boundless creativity. They are partners who will stand by your side with unwavering support and love, always seeking to understand and connect on a soul level. By embracing their sensitivity, valuing their dreams, and creating a nurturing and balanced relationship, you can ensure that your marriage with a Pisces is not only successful but also profoundly fulfilling.

CHAPTER TWO

PISCES 2025 HOROSCOPE

Overview Pisces 2025

Pisces (February 19 - March 20)

Dear Pisces, as we embark on the transformative journey of 2025, the celestial dance promises a year of profound spiritual growth, emotional healing, and inspired creativity for you. The cosmic energies align to support your path of self-discovery and empowerment, guiding you through the ebb and flow of life with your innate intuitive wisdom and compassionate heart.

The year commences with a powerful concentration of energy in your 12th house of spirituality, dreams, and inner transformation. The Sun, Mercury, and Venus converge in this mystical sector, urging you to turn inward and connect with your subconscious mind. Embrace this opportunity to release old patterns, fears, or limiting beliefs that may have hindered your progress. Saturn's presence in this house until March 1 provides the discipline and structure necessary to build a strong spiritual foundation. Engage in practices such as meditation, journaling, or creative visualization to tap into your intuition and gain clarity on your life's purpose.

In mid-January, the True Node shifts into your sign, signaling a powerful call to step into your authentic self and embrace your unique identity. This is a time to shed any masks or roles that no longer serve you and trust the wisdom of your heart. With the South Node in your opposite sign of Virgo, strive for balance and integration between your spiritual and practical worlds. You may find fulfillment in acts of service, healing, or mentorship, as you channel your empathy and compassion into the world.

February brings a significant shift as Saturn moves into Pisces on the 1st, followed by Venus on the 2nd. Saturn's entry into your sign until May 24 marks the beginning of a new 30-year cycle of growth and maturity. Embrace the challenges and opportunities for personal development that Saturn presents. Take responsibility for your life, set clear goals and boundaries, and cultivate the discipline and perseverance needed to manifest your dreams. Venus graces your sign until March 27, enhancing your charm, creativity, and ability to attract love and abundance. Use this period to express your unique talents, nurture relationships, and find joy in the simple pleasures of life.

The Total Lunar Eclipse in your 7th house of partnerships on March 14 brings a powerful opportunity for transformation and growth in your closest relationships. This is a time to release codependent patterns, assert your needs and boundaries, and cultivate deeper intimacy and trust with your loved ones. With Saturn's influence in your sign, you may need to confront fears or insecurities that have prevented true connection and vulnerability. Communications may also be emphasized as Mercury enters your sign on March 29.

On March 30, Neptune, your ruling planet, shifts into Aries, bringing a 14-year cycle of heightened intuition, spiritual growth, and inspired creativity to your 2nd house of values and resources. This transit encourages you to align your material world with your spiritual values, trust in the flow of the universe, and attract wealth and success through your unique gifts and talents. Embrace your dreams, visions, and ideals, and trust in the magic and mystery of life.

April 4 brings the first of three Saturn-Uranus sextiles in 2025, inspiring a harmonious blend of stability and innovation in your life. Embrace change and progress while maintaining a solid foundation. The second Saturn-Uranus sextile occurs on August 11, continuing the theme of balancing structure and flexibility. These transits provide opportunities for personal growth, unconventional solutions, and the manifestation of your long-term goals.

In late April, Pluto turns retrograde in your 11th house of friendships and social groups, initiating a period of reflection and re-evaluation in your connections with others. Assess the authenticity and quality of your relationships, releasing any that may be draining or toxic. Focus on cultivating a supportive network of individuals who share your values and aspirations.

May brings a brief preview of Saturn's influence in Aries as it shifts into your 2nd house from May 24 to September 1. This transit offers a glimpse of the forthcoming growth and challenges related to your values, self-worth, and material resources. Take stock of your life, assess your strengths and weaknesses, and begin establishing the structures necessary for long-term financial and emotional security.

The second half of the year emphasizes creativity, self-expression, and personal growth. Ceres' entry into your sign on August 11 and Sun's transit through Pisces from February 18 to March 20 highlight the importance of self-care, nurturance, and emotional well-being. Prioritize activities that bring you joy, rejuvenation, and a sense of inner peace.

On September 1, Saturn retrograde re-enters your sign, providing an opportunity to revisit and refine the lessons and growth you experienced earlier in the year. Reflect on your progress, make necessary adjustments, and continue building the foundation for your long-term success and fulfillment.

The Partial Solar Eclipse in your 2nd house on September 21 marks a powerful new beginning related to your values, resources, and self-worth. This is an ideal time to set intentions, make positive changes, and embrace opportunities for financial growth and prosperity. Trust in your abilities, talents, and the abundance the universe has to offer.

October 22 brings Neptune retrograde back into your sign, amplifying your intuition, creativity, and spiritual awareness. This transit encourages introspection, dream exploration, and the release of limiting beliefs or illusions. Embrace your imagination, trust your inner guidance, and allow your creativity to flow freely.

As the year draws to a close, Saturn's direct station in your sign on November 27 and Neptune's direct station on December 10 signify a period of renewed clarity, purpose, and momentum. Trust in the growth and lessons you've experienced throughout the year, and move forward with confidence and determination. Jupiter's biquintile to Pluto on November 30 supports positive transformations and the manifestation of your deepest desires.

Throughout 2025, Chiron's presence in your 2nd house of self-worth and resources encourages healing and growth in these areas. Embrace your unique value, talents, and contributions, and release any self-doubt or feelings of unworthiness. As you navigate the challenges and opportunities of the year, remember to practice self-compassion, maintain healthy boundaries, and trust in your inherent wisdom and resilience.

In conclusion, dear Pisces, 2025 promises to be a year of profound spiritual growth, emotional healing, and inspired creativity. The cosmic energies support your journey of self-discovery and empowerment, guiding you to align with your true purpose and manifest your deepest desires. Embrace the opportunities for personal development, cultivate meaningful relationships, and trust in the wisdom of the universe. With an open heart and a willing spirit, you have the power to create a life filled with magic, love, and abundant blessings. Trust in your path, stay true to your intuition, and embrace the transformative journey ahead.

January 2025

Overview Horoscope for the Month:

Dear Pisces, January 2025 is a month of profound spiritual growth and emotional healing for you. The year begins with a powerful stellium of planets in your 12th house of spirituality, dreams, and inner transformation, including the Sun, Mercury, Venus, and Saturn. This cosmic alignment is urging you to turn inward, connect with your subconscious mind, and release any old patterns, fears, or limiting beliefs that may be holding you back.

The New Moon in Aquarius on January 29th activates your 12th house, bringing a fresh start and new opportunities for spiritual awakening and inner growth. Set intentions for emotional healing, forgiveness, and letting go of the past. Trust your intuition and allow yourself to be guided by your dreams and inner wisdom.

Love:

In love, January 2025 is a time of deep emotional connection and spiritual intimacy for you, dear Pisces.

With Venus, the planet of love and relationships, traveling through your 12th house until February 2nd, you may find yourself craving a soul-level bond with your partner or seeking a relationship that transcends the physical realm.

If you're in a committed relationship, take time to connect with your partner on a deeper level through shared spiritual practices, heartfelt conversations, and acts of loving kindness. Be open and vulnerable about your feelings, fears, and dreams, and create a safe space for emotional healing and growth

If you're single, you may find yourself attracted to someone who shares your spiritual values and offers a sense of emotional depth and understanding. Trust your intuition and allow yourself to be guided towards meaningful connections that support your personal and spiritual growth.

Career:

In your career, January 2025 is a month of introspection and inner reflection for you, dear Pisces. With Saturn, the planet of responsibility and discipline, entering your 12th house on January 1st, you may find yourself questioning your current path and seeking a deeper sense of purpose and meaning in your work.

Take time to reassess your goals, values, and priorities, and make sure that your career aligns with your authentic self and soul's calling. Trust that the universe is guiding you towards your highest potential, even if the path is not always clear or easy.

If you're considering a career change or starting a new project, the New Moon in Aquarius on January 29th is a powerful time to set intentions and take inspired action towards your dreams. Trust your unique talents and abilities, and don't be afraid to think outside the box or take unconventional approaches to your work.

Finances:

In finances, January 2025 is a month of spiritual abundance and trust for you, dear Pisces. With Venus, the planet of money and resources, traveling through your 12th house until February 2nd, you are being called to release any fears or limiting beliefs around scarcity or lack, and to trust in the flow and provision of the universe.

Practice gratitude for the blessings in your life, and cultivate a mindset of abundance and generosity. Consider setting aside a portion of your income for charitable donations or acts of kindness that align with your spiritual values and beliefs.

On a deeper level, reflect on your relationship with money and any past wounds or traumas that may be blocking your financial flow. Practice forgiveness, self-love, and affirming your worthiness to receive all the good that life has to offer.

Health:

In health, January 2025 is a month of deep emotional healing and spiritual rejuvenation for you, dear Pisces. With the Sun, Mercury, and Venus all traveling through your 12th house of the subconscious mind, you may find yourself feeling more introspective, intuitive, and emotionally sensitive than usual.

Take time to rest, recharge, and connect with your inner world through practices like meditation, journaling, or creative visualization. Nourish your body with wholesome foods, plenty of water, and gentle exercise that supports your overall well-being.

On an emotional level, be gentle and compassionate with yourself as you navigate any old wounds, fears, or patterns that may arise. Seek out the support of trusted friends, therapists, or spiritual advisors who can offer guidance and a listening ear. Remember that true healing comes from within, and trust in the wisdom of your body, mind, and soul.

Travel:

In travel, January 2025 may bring opportunities for spiritual retreats, pilgrimages, or solo adventures that support your inner journey of self-discovery and growth. With Saturn entering your 12th house on January 1st, you may feel called to visit sacred sites, connect with nature, or explore new spiritual practices and traditions.

Consider taking a trip to a place that holds deep meaning and significance for you, such as a monastery, ashram, or natural wonder. Allow yourself to unplug from the distractions of daily life and immerse yourself in the beauty and wisdom of your surroundings.

If travel isn't possible or practical, find ways to create a sense of sacred space and inner retreat in your daily life. Take a nature walk, create a meditation corner in your home, or attend a local spiritual workshop or event that nourishes your soul.

Insights from the Stars:

The celestial energies of January 2025 are inviting you to dive deep into your inner world, dear Pisces, and to trust in the wisdom and guidance of your soul. With so many planets activating your 12th house of spirituality and the subconscious mind, this is a powerful time for inner growth, emotional healing, and spiritual transformation.

Embrace the journey of self-discovery and allow yourself to be guided by your intuition, dreams, and inner knowing. Trust that the universe is supporting you every step of the way, and that every challenge or obstacle is an opportunity for growth and awakening.

Remember that you are a divine being of light and love, and that your soul's purpose is to shine your unique gifts and talents in service to the world. Embrace your sensitivity, compassion, and creativity as the superpowers that they are, and trust in the magic and mystery of life.

Best Days of the Month:

- January 6th: First Quarter Moon in Aries - A burst of energy and motivation to take action on your dreams and goals.
- January 13th: Full Moon in Cancer - A time for emotional release, healing, and self-care.
- January 21st: Last Quarter Moon in Scorpio - An opportunity to let go of old patterns and beliefs that no longer serve you.
- January 29th: New Moon in Aquarius - A powerful time for setting intentions and planting seeds for the future, especially

related to your spiritual growth and inner journey.

- January 30th: Uranus Direct in Taurus - A shift towards greater freedom, innovation, and authentic self-expression in your communication and self-worth.

February 2025

Overview Horoscope for the Month:

Dear Pisces, February 2025 promises to be a month of profound spiritual growth, emotional healing, and personal transformation. With a powerful stellium of planets in your sign, including the Sun, Mercury, Saturn, and Neptune, you are being called to dive deep into your inner world and connect with your soul's true purpose. This is a time to release old patterns, heal past wounds, and embrace your unique gifts and talents.

The New Moon in your sign on February 27 brings a powerful opportunity for new beginnings and fresh starts. Set intentions for personal growth, creative expression, and spiritual awakening, and trust that the universe is supporting you every step of the way.

Love:

In matters of the heart, February 2025 invites you to deepen your connections and cultivate greater intimacy and vulnerability. With Venus entering your sign on the 2nd, you are radiating a magnetic and alluring energy that attracts soulful connections and heartfelt exchanges.

If you're in a committed partnership, this is a beautiful time to share your dreams, fears, and desires with your loved one, and to create a safe space for emotional healing and growth. Practice active listening, empathy, and unconditional love, and be willing to let go of any patterns or dynamics that no longer serve your highest good.

If you're single and seeking love, trust that the universe is guiding you towards relationships that align with your soul's path. Focus on cultivating a loving relationship with yourself first, and know that you deserve to be cherished, respected, and adored for all that you are.

Career:

In your professional life, February 2025 encourages you to align your work with your spiritual values and soul's purpose. With Saturn and Neptune activating your 12th house of inner growth and psychic abilities, you may feel called to explore career paths that involve healing, creativity, or service to others. Trust your intuition and inner guidance, and be open to unexpected opportunities and synchronicities that lead you towards your true calling.

If you're already in a fulfilling career, this is a wonderful time to infuse more meaning, purpose, and creativity into your work. Look for ways to make a positive impact on the world around you, and to use your unique gifts and talents in service of the greater good. Remember that your work is an extension of your soul's journey, and that every challenge or obstacle is an opportunity for growth and transformation.

Finances:

In financial matters, February 2025 invites you to cultivate a mindset of abundance, gratitude, and trust. With Jupiter and Uranus activating your 2nd house of values and resources, you are being called to align your material world with your spiritual beliefs and to attract wealth and prosperity through unconventional means.

Practice affirming your worthiness to receive all the good that life has to offer, and release any limiting beliefs or fears around scarcity or lack. Trust that the universe is always providing for your needs, and that every financial challenge is an opportunity to deepen your faith and surrender.

Consider exploring alternative sources of income or investment that align with your values and passions, and be open to unexpected windfalls or opportunities that come your way. Remember that true abundance flows from a heart of generosity, service, and love.

Health:

In matters of health and well-being, February 2025 encourages you to prioritize self-care, rest, and emotional healing. With the Sun, Mercury, and Neptune activating your 12th house of spirituality and solitude, you may feel more sensitive, intuitive, and introspective than usual. Honor your body's need for rest and relaxation, and create space in your schedule for activities that nourish your soul, such as meditation, journaling, or creative expression.

Pay attention to any physical symptoms or emotional triggers that arise, as they may be pointing you towards areas of your life that need healing or release. Practice self-compassion, forgiveness, and acceptance, and seek out the support of trusted healers or therapists who can guide you on your journey of wholeness.

Remember that true health and well-being come from a place of balance, harmony, and alignment with your soul's truth. Trust in the wisdom of your body, mind, and spirit, and know that you have the power to create a life of vitality, joy, and ease.

Travel:

In the realm of travel and adventure, February 2025 invites you to explore new spiritual practices, philosophies, or traditions that expand your consciousness and deepen your connection to the divine. With Saturn and Neptune activating your 12th house of inner growth and mystical experiences, you may feel called to embark on a pilgrimage, retreat, or vision quest that allows you to unplug from the distractions of daily life and connect with your higher self.

If physical travel is not possible or practical, consider exploring virtual workshops, online communities, or foreign films and books that introduce you to new cultures and ways of being. Remember that the greatest adventure is the journey within, and that every experience - whether near or far - is an opportunity for growth, learning, and transformation.

Insights from the Stars:

The cosmic energies of February 2025 are inviting you to embrace your spiritual path and trust in the wisdom of your soul, dear Pisces. With Saturn, Neptune, and the Full Moon Total Lunar Eclipse activating your sign, you are being called to release old patterns, beliefs, and identities that no longer serve your highest good, and to step into your true power and purpose.

This is a time to connect with your inner guidance, to listen to the whispers of your heart, and to trust in the magic and mystery of the universe. Know that you are exactly where you need to be, and that every challenge or obstacle is a sacred invitation to grow, heal, and evolve.

Remember that you are a divine being of love and light, and that your presence on this planet is a precious gift to the world. Embrace your sensitivity, creativity, and compassion as the superpowers that they are, and trust that you have the strength, wisdom, and resilience to navigate any storm.

Best Days of the Month:
- February 5: First Quarter Moon in Taurus - A grounding and stabilizing energy that supports practical action and manifestation.
- February 12: Full Moon Total Lunar Eclipse in Leo - A powerful time for releasing old patterns and stepping into your authentic self-expression.
- February 14: Mercury enters Pisces - Enhancing your intuition, creativity, and emotional intelligence.
- February 18: Sun enters Pisces - Marking the beginning of a new solar cycle and fresh starts in your personal life.
- February 23: Mars Direct in Cancer - Supporting forward movement and

emotional clarity in your home and family life.

- February 27: New Moon in Pisces - A potent time for setting intentions and planting seeds for your dreams and aspirations.

March 2025

Overview Horoscope for the Month:

March 2025 brings a powerful wave of spiritual awakening and personal transformation for you, dear Pisces. With a potent stellium of planets in your sign, including Saturn entering Pisces on March 1st, you are being called to dive deep into your inner world, confront your fears and limitations, and embrace your true path and purpose. This is a time of profound self-discovery, healing, and growth, as you release old patterns and beliefs that no longer serve you and step into a new chapter of your life.

The New Moon in Aries on March 29th falls in your 2nd house of values, finances, and self-worth, marking a fresh start in your relationship with abundance and prosperity. Set clear intentions for financial growth, positive self-talk, and aligning your resources with your spiritual values and goals.

Love:

In matters of the heart, March 2025 invites you to cultivate deeper intimacy, vulnerability, and spiritual connection with your loved ones. With Venus retrograde in Aries from March 1st to 27th, you may find yourself revisiting past relationships, healing old wounds, or gaining closure on unresolved emotional issues. Use this time to reflect on your patterns, needs, and desires in love, and to practice self-love and compassion.

When Venus re-enters your sign on March 27th, followed by the New Moon in Aries on March 29th, you may experience a renewed sense of clarity, confidence, and magnetism in your relationships. Be open to new connections or rekindled romance that align with your authentic self and highest path.

Career:

In your professional life, March 2025 marks a significant turning point, as Saturn enters your sign on March 1st, initiating a new 2.5-year cycle of career growth, responsibility, and mastery. You are being called to take a serious look at your long-term goals, develop a solid plan of action, and put in the hard work and discipline needed to achieve your dreams.

At the same time, with Mercury retrograde in your sign from March 15th to April 7th, you may need to revisit old projects, revise your communication strategies, or rethink your approach to work. Trust your intuition and allow yourself the time and space to make any necessary adjustments or course corrections.

Finances:

The New Moon in Aries on March 29th brings a powerful opportunity to set intentions and take action towards your financial goals and aspirations. With Uranus and Neptune aligning in your 2nd house of money and resources, you may experience sudden breakthroughs, unexpected windfalls, or innovative ideas for increasing your income and prosperity.

At the same time, be mindful of any tendencies towards overspending, financial risk-taking, or unrealistic expectations. Stay grounded in your values, budget wisely, and trust that the universe will provide for your needs as you align your resources with your spiritual path and purpose.

Health:

With the Sun, Mercury, Venus, Saturn, and Neptune all activating your 12th house of spirituality, solitude, and inner work, March 2025 is a deeply introspective and transformative month for your physical, emotional, and spiritual well-being. You may feel more sensitive, intuitive, and attuned to the subtler realms of your being, and may need more time alone to rest, recharge, and connect with your inner guidance.

Prioritize self-care practices that nourish your mind, body, and soul, such as meditation, dream work, energy healing, or creative expression. Be gentle with yourself as you navigate any challenges or obstacles that arise, and trust that every experience is an opportunity for growth, healing, and self-discovery.

Travel:

With so much planetary activity in your 12th house of spirituality and inner work, March 2025 may be a more inward-focused month for you, with less emphasis on physical travel or external adventures. However, this is a powerful time for inner journeys, spiritual retreats, or immersive experiences that allow you to connect with your higher self and the mysteries of the universe.

If you do feel called to travel, trust your intuition and allow yourself to be guided towards destinations or experiences that support your spiritual growth and transformation. Be open to synchronicities, divine guidance, and unexpected opportunities for healing and awakening.

Insights from the Stars:

The cosmic energies of March 2025 are inviting you to embrace your spiritual path, trust your inner wisdom, and surrender to the transformative power of love and grace. With Saturn entering your sign for the first time in 29 years, you are embarking on a profound journey of self-mastery, responsibility, and personal growth. Embrace the challenges and opportunities that arise as sacred lessons and tests of your strength, faith, and resilience.

At the same time, with the Total Lunar Eclipse in Virgo on March 14th activating your 7th house of partnerships and the Partial Solar Eclipse in Aries on March 29th igniting your 2nd house of self-worth, you are being called to release any limiting beliefs, toxic relationships, or unhealthy attachments that are holding you back from your true potential and prosperity. Trust in the power of endings and beginnings, and know that the universe is conspiring to support your highest good and evolution.

Best Days of the Month:
- March 1st: Saturn enters Pisces - The beginning of a new 2.5-year cycle of personal growth, responsibility, and self-mastery.
- March 14th: Full Moon Total Lunar Eclipse in Virgo - A powerful portal for releasing old patterns, healing

relationships, and embracing a new level of wholeness and balance.

- March 27th: Venus retrogrades back into Pisces - A time for deepening self-love, compassion, and emotional healing.
- March 29th: New Moon Partial Solar Eclipse in Aries - A potent opportunity to set intentions and take action towards your financial goals and aspirations.
- March 30th: Neptune enters Aries - The beginning of a new 14-year cycle of spiritual awakening, creative inspiration, and intuitive guidance.

April 2025

Overview Horoscope for the Month:

Dear Pisces, April 2025 is a month of profound spiritual growth, emotional healing, and positive transformation. The cosmic energies are supporting your journey of self-discovery and inner awakening, guiding you towards a deeper connection with your intuition, creativity, and soul's purpose.

The month begins with Mercury and Venus in your sign, enhancing your communication skills, creativity, and magnetism. This is a wonderful time to express your ideas, share your gifts, and attract positive connections and opportunities into your life.

The New Moon in Taurus on April 27 illuminates your 3rd house of learning, communication, and self-expression. Set intentions for expanding your knowledge, honing your skills, and sharing your unique perspective with the world. Trust in the power of your voice and the value of your ideas.

Love:

In matters of the heart, April 2025 invites you to deepen your emotional connections and cultivate greater intimacy and authenticity in your relationships. With Venus in your sign until the 30th, you are radiating a warm, compassionate, and attractive energy that draws others to you. Use this time to express your affection, share your desires, and create a safe space for emotional bonding and growth.

If you're in a committed partnership, the Full Moon in Libra on April 12 highlights your 8th house of deep emotional bonds and shared resources. This is a powerful time to release any fears, resentments, or blocks to intimacy, and to recommit to your love and trust for one another. Be open to vulnerable conversations and transformative experiences that bring you closer together.

If you're single, be open to new connections and synchronicities that align with your values and aspirations. Focus on cultivating a loving relationship with yourself first, and trust that the right person will come into your life at the perfect time.

Career:

In your professional life, April 2025 encourages you to align your work with your spiritual values and inner purpose. With Saturn forming a harmonious sextile to Uranus on the 4th, you may experience unexpected opportunities, innovative ideas, or breakthroughs in your career path. Trust your intuition and be open to unconventional approaches or alternative solutions that allow you to express your unique talents and perspective.

At the same time, with Mercury and Venus in your sign for most of the month, you have a powerful opportunity to communicate your ideas, collaborate with others, and attract positive attention and recognition for your work. Use your creativity, compassion, and intuition to make a meaningful impact and inspire others with your vision.

Finances:

In financial matters, April 2025 invites you to cultivate a mindset of abundance, gratitude, and trust. With Jupiter and Pluto forming a harmonious aspect mid-month, you may experience unexpected windfalls, opportunities for growth, or the resolution of long-standing financial issues. Practice affirming your worthiness to receive all the good that life has to offer, and release any fears or limiting beliefs around scarcity or lack.

At the same time, be mindful of any tendencies towards overspending or financial risk-taking. Stay grounded in your values, budget wisely, and trust that the universe will provide for your needs as you align your resources with your spiritual path and purpose.

Health:

In matters of health and well-being, April 2025 encourages you to prioritize self-care, rest, and emotional healing. With the Sun and Mercury in your sign for the first part of the month, you may feel more energized, expressive, and mentally active than usual. Use this time to engage in activities that stimulate your mind, body, and soul, such as learning a new skill, trying a new form of exercise, or exploring a creative hobby.

At the same time, be mindful of any tendencies towards overextending yourself or neglecting your physical and emotional needs. Make sure to carve out time for relaxation, meditation, and introspection, especially around the Full Moon in Libra on April 12. Listen to your body's wisdom and trust your intuition when it comes to self-care and healing.

Travel:

In the realm of travel and adventure, April 2025 may bring opportunities for short trips, learning experiences, or connections with people from different backgrounds and cultures. With Mercury and Venus activating your 3rd house of communication and learning, you may feel a strong desire to expand your mind, broaden your horizons, and engage in stimulating conversations and exchanges.

If travel is not possible or practical, consider exploring online courses, workshops, or virtual communities that allow you to connect with like-minded individuals and gain new insights and perspectives. Be open to synchronicities and unexpected opportunities that align with your interests and aspirations.

Insights from the Stars:

The cosmic energies of April 2025 are inviting you to embrace your spiritual path and trust in the wisdom of your soul, dear Pisces. With Saturn forming a harmonious sextile to Uranus on the 4th, you are being called to balance structure and innovation, responsibility and freedom, in pursuit of your highest purpose and potential. Trust that the challenges and opportunities that arise are all part of your soul's journey of growth and evolution.

At the same time, with Jupiter and Pluto forming a harmonious aspect mid-month, you have a powerful opportunity to transform your beliefs, expand your consciousness, and tap into your inner power and resilience. Trust in the universe's ability to support and guide you, and know that every experience is a chance to learn, heal, and evolve.

Best Days of the Month:

- April 4: Saturn sextile Uranus - A day of unexpected opportunities, innovative solutions, and breakthroughs in your career and life path.
- April 7: Mercury Direct in Pisces - Clarity and forward movement in your communication, self-expression, and mental pursuits.
- April 12: Full Moon in Libra - A powerful time for releasing fears, healing relationships, and cultivating balance and harmony in your emotional and financial life.
- April 21: Saturn conjunct True Node - A significant alignment of your karmic path and spiritual purpose, inviting you to step into your power and leadership.
- April 27: New Moon in Taurus - A potent time for setting intentions and planting seeds for growth and abundance in your communication, learning, and self-expression.

May 2025

Overview Horoscope for the Month:

Dear Pisces, May 2025 promises to be a month of personal growth, spiritual insight, and positive change. The cosmic energies are supporting your journey of self-discovery and inner transformation, encouraging you to embrace your unique talents, express your creativity, and connect with your higher purpose.

The month begins with the Sun in Taurus, illuminating your 3rd house of communication, learning, and self-expression. This is a wonderful time to explore new ideas, engage in stimulating conversations, and share your knowledge and insights with others. Trust in the power of your voice and the value of your unique perspective.

The New Moon in Gemini on May 26 activates your 4th house of home, family, and emotional foundations. Set intentions for creating a nurturing and supportive living space, strengthening your family bonds, and cultivating a deeper sense of inner peace and security. Trust that you have the resilience and adaptability to navigate any challenges or changes that arise in your personal life.

Love:

In matters of the heart, May 2025 invites you to cultivate greater harmony, balance, and mutual understanding in your relationships. With Venus moving through Aries and Taurus this month, you may feel a strong desire for both independence and stability in your connections. Take time to clarify your needs and boundaries, while also being open to compromise and cooperation with your loved ones.

If you're in a committed partnership, the Full Moon in Scorpio on May 12 illuminates your 9th house of adventure, growth, and higher learning. This is a powerful time to explore new experiences together, challenge your assumptions, and deepen your emotional and spiritual bond. Be open to transformative conversations and revelations that bring you closer to your shared truth and purpose.

If you're single, focus on cultivating a loving and accepting relationship with yourself first. Engage in activities that bring you joy, confidence, and a sense of adventure. Trust that the right person will come into your life when you're radiating your most authentic and vibrant self.

Career:

In your professional life, May 2025 encourages you to tap into your creativity, intuition, and communication skills to make progress and achieve your goals. With Mercury moving through Taurus and Gemini this month, you have a powerful opportunity to express your ideas, collaborate with others, and adapt to changing circumstances in your work environment.

At the same time, with Pluto retrograde in your 11th house of networking and future vision, you may need to reassess your long-term goals, alliances, and strategies for success. Be willing to let go of any outdated plans or associations that no longer align with your values and aspirations. Trust your inner guidance and be open to unexpected opportunities that come your way.

Finances:

In financial matters, May 2025 invites you to cultivate a mindset of abundance, gratitude, and practical planning. With the Sun and Mercury moving through your 2nd house of values and resources, you have a wonderful opportunity to reassess your priorities, create a realistic budget, and make informed decisions about your money and possessions.

At the same time, with Jupiter and Uranus forming harmonious aspects this month, you may experience unexpected windfalls, opportunities for growth, or innovative ideas for increasing your income and prosperity. Stay open to new possibilities and be willing to take calculated risks that align with your long-term vision and values.

Health:

In matters of health and well-being, May 2025 encourages you to prioritize self-care, mindfulness, and emotional healing. With the Sun and Mercury moving through grounding Taurus, you may feel a strong desire for stability, comfort, and sensory pleasure. Take time to enjoy nourishing meals, spend time in nature, and engage in activities that bring you a sense of peace and relaxation.

At the same time, be mindful of any tendencies towards overindulgence or avoidance of emotional issues. The Full Moon in Scorpio on May 12 invites you to confront any fears, resentments, or hidden wounds that may be impacting your physical and mental health. Seek the support of trusted healers, therapists, or spiritual practices to help you release and transform any heavy emotions or limiting beliefs.

Travel:

In the realm of travel and adventure, May 2025 may bring opportunities for short trips, cultural exchanges, or educational pursuits that expand your mind and broaden your horizons. With Mercury moving through your 3rd house of communication and learning, you may feel a strong curiosity and desire to explore new ideas, places, and perspectives.

If travel is not possible or practical, consider exploring online courses, virtual tours, or foreign language apps that allow you to connect with different cultures and ways of life. Be open to synchronicities and unexpected encounters that bring fresh insights and inspiration into your world.

Insights from the Stars:

The cosmic energies of May 2025 are inviting you to embrace your authentic self, trust your inner wisdom, and share your unique gifts with the world. With Saturn moving into Aries mid-month, you are entering a new 2.5-year cycle of personal growth, self-assertion, and bold action. Embrace the challenges and opportunities that arise as chances to develop your strength, confidence, and leadership skills.

At the same time, with Jupiter and Neptune forming harmonious aspects this month, you have a powerful opportunity to connect with your spiritual purpose, creative inspiration, and highest ideals. Trust in the universe's ability to guide and support you, and know that your dreams and visions have the power to manifest into reality.

Best Days of the Month:
- May 4: First Quarter Moon in Leo - A day of creative self-expression, joyful play, and heartfelt connections.
- May 12: Full Moon in Scorpio - A powerful time for releasing fears, transforming relationships, and embracing your inner truth and power.
- May 18: Jupiter sextile Chiron - A healing and expansive aspect that supports emotional healing, spiritual growth, and the alignment of your beliefs and actions.
- May 24: Saturn enters Aries - The beginning of a new cycle of personal responsibility, self-assertion, and bold leadership in your life.
- May 26: New Moon in Gemini - A potent time for setting intentions and planting seeds for positive change in your home, family, and emotional foundations.

June 2025

Overview Horoscope for the Month:

Dear Pisces, June 2025 brings a mix of spiritual growth, emotional healing, and new beginnings. The month starts with Venus entering your 4th house of home and family on June 6th, encouraging you to focus on creating a nurturing and harmonious living environment. This is a wonderful time to connect with loved ones, engage in family activities, and find peace and comfort in your personal space.

The Full Moon in Sagittarius on June 11th illuminates your 10th house of career and public reputation, bringing a sense of completion or culmination to your professional goals and aspirations. Trust in your abilities and the progress you've made, and be open to new opportunities for growth and recognition.

Love:

In matters of the heart, June 2025 invites you to cultivate deeper emotional intimacy and vulnerability in your relationships. With Venus in your 4th house from June 6th to July 4th, you may feel a stronger desire for security, commitment, and familial bonds. Take time to nurture your closest connections, express your affection and appreciation, and create a safe space for open and honest communication.

If you're in a committed partnership, the Full Moon in Sagittarius on June 11th may bring a significant realization or turning point in your relationship. Use this energy to have honest and expansive conversations about your shared dreams, values, and long-term goals. Be willing to compromise and adapt as needed, while staying true to your own needs and desires.

If you're single, focus on cultivating a loving and accepting relationship with yourself first. Engage in activities that bring you joy, peace, and a sense of belonging. Trust that the right person will come into your life when you're radiating your most authentic and compassionate self.

Career:

In your professional life, June 2025 encourages you to align your work with your spiritual values and inner purpose. With Mars entering Virgo on June 17th and activating your 7th house of partnerships and collaborations, you may find new opportunities for growth and success through teamwork, networking, and cooperative efforts. Trust your intuition and be open to unconventional or innovative approaches that allow you to express your unique skills and perspective.

The Full Moon in Sagittarius on June 11th may bring a culmination or breakthrough in your career path, helping you to see the bigger picture and align your goals with your higher purpose. Stay focused on your long-term vision, while also being adaptable and responsive to changing circumstances.

Finances:

In financial matters, June 2025 invites you to cultivate a mindset of abundance, gratitude, and practical planning. With Venus in your 4th house, you may find greater security and stability in your material world, especially through investments in property, home improvements, or family resources. Be mindful of your spending habits and focus on creating a solid foundation for your long-term financial goals.

At the same time, trust in the universe's ability to provide for your needs and desires, and be open to unexpected sources of income or support. Practice generosity and sharing with others, knowing that the more you give, the more you will receive in return.

Health:

In matters of health and well-being, June 2025 encourages you to prioritize self-care, rest, and emotional healing. With the Sun in Cancer from June 20th onwards, you may feel more sensitive, intuitive, and attuned to your inner world. Take time to nurture yourself through gentle activities like meditation, nature walks, or creative pursuits that allow you to express your feelings and release any stress or tension.

Pay attention to your physical health as well, especially around the Full Moon in Sagittarius on June 11th. Make sure to get enough sleep, eat nourishing foods, and engage in regular exercise or movement that helps you feel strong, flexible, and energized.

Travel:

In the realm of travel and adventure, June 2025 may bring opportunities for short trips, family vacations, or exploring new horizons close to home. With Mercury entering Cancer on June 26th, you may feel a stronger desire to connect with your roots, visit familiar places, or learn more about your ancestral heritage.

If travel is not possible or practical, consider exploring new cultures, philosophies, or belief systems through books, movies, or online resources. Be open to expanding your mind and heart through learning, dialogue, and self-reflection.

Insights from the Stars:

The cosmic energies of June 2025 are inviting you to embrace your emotional depth, intuitive wisdom, and spiritual purpose. With Neptune, your ruling planet, in harmonious aspect to Saturn and Uranus this month, you have a powerful opportunity to ground your dreams and visions into practical reality, while also staying open to divine guidance and unexpected opportunities.

Trust in the journey of your soul, and know that every challenge or obstacle is an opportunity for growth, healing, and self-discovery. Stay connected to your inner truth, your compassion for others, and your faith in the universe, and you will navigate this month with grace, resilience, and wisdom.

Best Days of the Month:
- June 6th: Venus enters Cancer - A supportive influence for emotional bonding, family harmony, and creating a nurturing home environment.
- June 11th: Full Moon in Sagittarius - A powerful time for expanding your vision, aligning your goals with your higher purpose, and celebrating your achievements and progress.

- June 18th: Jupiter trine True Node - A fortunate aspect for spiritual growth, meaningful connections, and aligning your path with your soul's evolutionary journey.
- June 25th: New Moon in Cancer - A potent time for setting intentions and planting seeds for emotional healing, family unity, and creating a secure and loving foundation for your life.
- June 26th: Mercury enters Cancer - A helpful influence for heartfelt communication, emotional intelligence, and expressing your feelings with clarity and compassion.

July 2025

Overview Horoscope for the Month:

Dear Pisces, July 2025 is a month of personal growth, creative expression, and spiritual exploration. The cosmic energies are supporting your journey of self-discovery and empowering you to embrace your unique talents and desires.

The month begins with Mars entering Leo on July 22nd, igniting your 6th house of work, health, and daily routines. This transit brings a burst of energy and enthusiasm to your everyday life, encouraging you to take bold action towards your goals and prioritize your well-being.

The New Moon in Leo on July 24th further amplifies this theme, providing a powerful opportunity to set intentions and initiate new projects related to your job, self-improvement, or health regimen. Trust in your abilities and let your passion and creativity guide you forward.

Love:

In matters of the heart, July 2025 invites you to express your affection and desires with confidence and authenticity. With Venus moving through Gemini and Cancer this month, you may find yourself attracted to intelligent, emotionally attuned, and nurturing partners who appreciate your depth and sensitivity.

If you're in a committed relationship, the Full Moon in Capricorn on July 10th illuminates your 11th house of friendships and social networks, highlighting the importance of maintaining a balance between your romantic partnership and your connections with friends and community. Take time to nurture your bond with your partner while also cultivating supportive and inspiring friendships.

If you're single, focus on engaging in activities and environments that align with your interests and values. Trust that your authentic self-expression and openness to new experiences will attract compatible and meaningful connections.

Career:

In your professional life, July 2025 encourages you to bring your creativity, intuition, and dedication to your work. With Mars in Leo from July 22nd onwards, you have a powerful opportunity to showcase your unique talents, take on leadership roles, and make significant progress in your career.

However, with Mercury retrograde in Leo from July 18th to August 11th, you may need to review, revise, or reconsider certain projects or plans. Use this time to reassess your goals, refine your skills, and address any challenges or obstacles with patience and perseverance.

Finances:

In financial matters, July 2025 emphasizes the importance of balancing short-term desires with long-term security. With Venus in Gemini until July 30th, you may be tempted to indulge in impulsive purchases or risky investments. Stay mindful of your spending habits and focus on creating a stable and sustainable financial foundation.

At the same time, trust in the abundance of the universe and remain open to unexpected opportunities for growth and prosperity. Align your financial decisions with your values and aspirations, and be willing to invest in your own development and well-being.

Health:

In matters of health and well-being, July 2025 encourages you to prioritize self-care, mindfulness, and physical vitality. With Mars in Leo activating your 6th house of health and wellness, you have a strong motivation to improve your fitness, nutrition, and daily habits.

Take time to engage in activities that bring you joy, creativity, and a sense of accomplishment. Whether it's dancing, playing sports, or pursuing a passion project, find ways to express your energy and enthusiasm in a healthy and fulfilling manner.

Travel:

In the realm of travel and adventure, July 2025 may bring opportunities for short trips, cultural exploration, or learning experiences that expand your mind and broaden your horizons. With Mercury and Venus moving through curious Gemini, you may feel a strong desire to connect with new people, ideas, and environments.

If travel is not possible or practical, consider exploring your local surroundings with fresh eyes and an open mind. Engage in activities that stimulate your intellect, creativity, and sense of wonder, such as attending workshops, trying new hobbies, or connecting with people from diverse backgrounds.

Insights from the Stars:

The cosmic energies of July 2025 are inviting you to embrace your personal power, creativity, and spiritual wisdom. With Chiron retrograde in Aries from July 30th onwards, you have an opportunity to heal any wounds or insecurities related to your self-expression, leadership abilities, or pioneering spirit.

Trust in the unique gifts and perspectives you bring to the world, and don't be afraid to take risks or stand out from the crowd. Your sensitivity, compassion, and intuition are your greatest strengths, guiding you towards your highest path and purpose.

Best Days of the Month:
- July 2nd: First Quarter Moon in Libra - A time for harmonizing your relationships, finding balance, and collaborating with others towards a common goal.
- July 10th: Full Moon in Capricorn - An opportunity to celebrate your achievements, release limiting beliefs, and align your ambitions with your soul's purpose.
- July 19th: Jupiter quintile Chiron - A transformative aspect that supports healing,

growth, and the expression of your unique talents and abilities.

- July 24th: New Moon in Leo - A powerful time for setting intentions, initiating creative projects, and expressing your authentic self with confidence and joy.
- July 30th: Venus enters Cancer - A supportive influence for emotional connection, intuitive understanding, and nurturing your closest relationships.

August 2025

Overview Horoscope for the Month:

Dear Pisces, August 2025 is a month of emotional healing, creative inspiration, and spiritual growth. The cosmic energies are supporting your journey of self-discovery and inner transformation, encouraging you to trust your intuition, express your unique talents, and connect with your higher purpose.

The month begins with a powerful Full Moon in Aquarius on August 9th, illuminating your 12th house of spirituality, intuition, and inner growth. This lunation brings a culmination or revelation to your spiritual path, helping you to release old patterns, heal past wounds, and align with your soul's deepest truth and wisdom.

The New Moon in Virgo on August 23rd activates your 7th house of partnerships and relationships, marking a new beginning or fresh start in your connections with others. Set intentions for creating more balance, harmony, and mutual support in your relationships, and be open to new opportunities for collaboration and growth.

Love:

In matters of the heart, August 2025 invites you to deepen your emotional intimacy, vulnerability, and authenticity in your relationships. With Venus moving through Leo and Virgo this month, you may find yourself attracted to confident, expressive, and detail-oriented partners who appreciate your depth, sensitivity, and dedication.

If you're in a committed relationship, the Full Moon in Aquarius on August 9th may bring a shift or awakening in your spiritual connection with your partner. Take time to explore your shared beliefs, values, and aspirations, and be open to new ways of understanding and supporting each other's growth and evolution.

If you're single, focus on cultivating a loving and compassionate relationship with yourself first. Engage in activities that bring you joy, creativity, and a sense of purpose, and trust that your authentic self-expression will attract aligned and compatible connections.

Career:

In your professional life, August 2025 encourages you to align your work with your spiritual values and inner purpose. With the Sun and Mercury moving through Leo and Virgo this month, you have a powerful opportunity to showcase your unique talents, take on leadership roles, and make meaningful contributions to your field or community.

However, with Uranus retrograde in Gemini from August 6th onwards, you may need to navigate unexpected changes, challenges, or disruptions in your work environment. Stay flexible, adaptable, and open to new ideas and approaches, while also staying true to your core values and long-term goals.

Finances:

In financial matters, August 2025 emphasizes the importance of practical planning, organization, and wise management of your resources. With the New Moon in Virgo on August 23rd, you have an opportunity to set intentions and take action towards your financial goals, such as creating a budget, paying off debts, or investing in your future security.

At the same time, trust in the abundance of the universe and remain open to unexpected sources of income or support. Focus on aligning your financial decisions with your spiritual values and aspirations, and be willing to share your resources and talents with others in a way that feels meaningful and fulfilling.

Health:

In matters of health and well-being, August 2025 encourages you to prioritize self-care, mindfulness, and emotional healing. With the Full Moon in Aquarius on August 9th, you may experience a release or breakthrough in your mental health, helping you to let go of old patterns of stress, anxiety, or self-doubt.

Take time to engage in practices that nourish your mind, body, and soul, such as meditation, yoga, or creative expression. Pay attention to your physical health as well, especially around the New Moon in Virgo on August 23rd, which supports healthy habits, routines, and self-improvement.

Travel:

In the realm of travel and adventure, August 2025 may bring opportunities for spiritual retreats, workshops, or experiences that expand your consciousness and deepen your connection to the divine. With Venus and Mars moving through Leo, you may feel a strong desire to explore new horizons, express your creativity, and connect with like-minded individuals who share your passion for growth and transformation.

If travel is not possible or practical, consider exploring online courses, virtual events, or local communities that align with your interests and aspirations. Be open to new ideas, perspectives, and experiences that challenge and inspire you to grow beyond your comfort zone.

Insights from the Stars:

The cosmic energies of August 2025 are inviting you to embrace your spiritual path, creative power, and emotional wisdom. With Saturn retrograde in Pisces from August 1st onwards, you have an opportunity to review, refine, and recommit to your long-term goals and aspirations, while also staying open to divine guidance and unexpected opportunities.

Trust in the journey of your soul, and know that every challenge or obstacle is an opportunity for growth, healing, and self-discovery. Stay connected to your inner truth, your compassion for others, and your faith in the universe, and you will navigate this month with grace, resilience, and wisdom.

Best Days of the Month:

- August 3rd: Uranus quintile True Node - A transformative aspect that supports spiritual growth, innovative solutions, and aligning your path with your soul's evolutionary journey.

- August 9th: Full Moon in Aquarius - A powerful time for releasing old patterns, awakening to new insights, and connecting with your higher purpose and vision.
- August 11th: Saturn sextile Uranus - A harmonious influence that supports grounded change, practical innovation, and integrating your spiritual wisdom with your everyday life.
- August 23rd: New Moon in Virgo - A potent time for setting intentions and planting seeds for personal growth, healthy routines, and meaningful partnerships.
- August 28th: Uranus sextile Neptune - A highly intuitive and imaginative aspect that supports creative breakthroughs, spiritual insights, and compassionate action.

September 2025

Overview Horoscope for the Month:

Dear Pisces, September 2025 is a month of profound spiritual awakening, emotional healing, and personal transformation. The cosmic energies are supporting your journey of self-discovery and inner growth, urging you to connect with your intuition, release old patterns, and align with your soul's true purpose.

The month begins with a significant shift as Saturn retrograde re-enters your sign on September 1st. This transit invites you to revisit and refine the lessons and growth you experienced earlier in the year, particularly around personal responsibility, self-discipline, and long-term goals. Embrace this opportunity to build a stronger foundation for your future and trust in the wisdom of divine timing.

The Full Moon Total Lunar Eclipse in your sign on September 7th marks a powerful culmination and release in your personal journey of self-discovery and transformation. This lunation brings heightened emotions, revelations, and a call to let go of any limiting beliefs, patterns, or relationships that no longer serve your highest good. Trust in the process of release and renewal, and have faith in the new beginnings that await you.

Love:

In matters of the heart, September 2025 emphasizes the importance of emotional authenticity, vulnerability, and spiritual connection in your relationships. With Venus entering practical and detail-oriented Virgo on September 19th, you may find yourself attracted to partners who offer stability, reliability, and a shared sense of purpose.

If you're in a committed relationship, the Partial Solar Eclipse in Virgo on September 21st activates your 7th house of partnerships, marking a significant new chapter in your relationship dynamics. Use this energetic portal to set intentions for greater harmony, equality, and mutual growth in your union. Be open to having honest conversations about your needs, desires, and shared vision for the future.

If you're single, focus on cultivating a loving relationship with yourself first. Engage in practices that nurture your self-worth, self-care, and inner peace. Trust that by radiating your authentic light and vibration, you will attract aligned and supportive connections into your life.

Career:

In your professional life, September 2025 encourages you to align your work with your spiritual values and soul's calling. With Mars entering deep and transformative Scorpio on September 22nd, you may feel a strong drive to pursue projects or roles that allow you to make a meaningful impact and facilitate positive change.

However, with Mercury stationing retrograde in Libra on September 21st, you may need to review, revise, or renegotiate certain contracts, agreements, or collaborative efforts in your work. Use this time to reassess your professional goals, communicate clearly, and make any necessary adjustments that support your long-term success and well-being.

Trust your intuition and be open to unexpected opportunities or insights that arise during this time. Remember that your work is an extension of your spiritual path, and that every challenge is an opportunity for growth and self-discovery.

Finances:

In financial matters, September 2025 emphasizes the importance of aligning your resources and investments with your values and long-term goals. The

New Moon in Virgo on September 21st brings a powerful opportunity to set intentions and create practical strategies for financial growth, security, and abundance.

Trust in the universe's ability to provide for your needs and have faith in your own resourcefulness and resilience. Be open to new sources of income or innovative ways to manage your finances, but also be discerning and grounded in your choices. Focus on creating a solid foundation for your material world, while also practicing generosity and detachment.

Health:

In matters of health and well-being, September 2025 invites you to prioritize self-care, rest, and emotional processing. The Full Moon Total Lunar Eclipse in your sign on September 7th may bring intense feelings, revelations, or physical symptoms to the surface. Honor your body's wisdom and take time to nurture yourself with gentle practices like meditation, nature walks, or creative expression.

Pay attention to any persistent health issues or emotional patterns that may require professional support or targeted healing work. Trust in the power of vulnerability and ask for help when needed. Remember that true wellness involves a holistic balance of mind, body, and spirit.

Travel:

In the realm of travel and adventure, September 2025 may bring opportunities for spiritual pilgrimages, transformative workshops, or immersive experiences that expand your consciousness. With Jupiter in harmonious alignment with your North Node on September 3rd, you may feel called to explore new horizons, connect with like-minded souls, and align your path with your soul's evolutionary journey.

If physical travel is not possible, consider embarking on inner journeys through practices like shamanic journeying, lucid dreaming, or deep meditation. Seek out teachers, mentors, or wisdom traditions that resonate with your spiritual curiosity and desire for growth.

Insights from the Stars:

The cosmic energies of September 2025 are inviting you to embrace your spiritual authority, emotional authenticity, and creative power. With the Full Moon Total Lunar Eclipse in your sign on September 7th, you are being called to step into your full radiance, release the past, and claim your soul's true path forward.

Trust in the journey of your heart, even when the way seems uncertain or challenging. Know that every experience is a catalyst for your growth and that your sensitivity and intuition are your greatest allies. Stay anchored in your spiritual practice, surround yourself with loving support, and have faith in the unfolding of your divine destiny.

Best Days of the Month:

- September 3rd: Jupiter trine True Node - A powerful alignment that supports spiritual growth, fated encounters, and aligning your path with your soul's evolutionary purpose.
- September 7th: Full Moon Total Lunar Eclipse in Pisces - A profound portal for releasing the past, claiming your power, and birthing a new chapter in your personal journey.
- September 14th: Last Quarter Moon in Gemini - A supportive influence for releasing mental clutter, integrating insights, and finding clarity in your communication and ideas.
- September 21st: New Moon Partial Solar Eclipse in Virgo - A potent time for setting intentions and planting seeds for positive change in your relationships, health, and work.

- September 29th: First Quarter Moon in Capricorn - A helpful energy for taking practical steps, setting realistic goals, and building a solid foundation for your dreams and aspirations.

October 2025

Overview Horoscope for the Month:

Dear Pisces, October 2025 is a month of deep emotional transformation, spiritual growth, and personal empowerment. With the Sun in Libra illuminating your 8th house of intimacy, shared resources, and psychological healing until October 22nd, you are called to confront your fears, explore your inner depths, and release old patterns that no longer serve your highest good.

The New Moon in Libra on October 21st brings a powerful opportunity to set intentions and plant seeds related to emotional healing, financial partnerships, and spiritual regeneration. Trust your intuition and be open to unexpected breakthroughs and revelations.

On October 22nd, the Sun shifts into Scorpio, followed by the ingress of Mercury and Venus later in the month. This energy activates your 9th house of higher learning, philosophy, and adventure, inviting you to expand your mind, seek new experiences, and connect with your inner truth and wisdom.

Love:

In matters of the heart, October 2025 emphasizes the importance of emotional authenticity, vulnerability, and deep soul connections. With Venus moving through Libra and Scorpio this month, you may find yourself attracted to partners who challenge you to grow, transform, and explore the deeper dimensions of love and intimacy.

If you're in a committed relationship, the Full Moon in Aries on October 6th illuminates your 2nd house of values, self-worth, and personal resources. Use this energy to have honest conversations with your partner about your needs, desires, and shared values. Be open to finding creative solutions and compromises that honor both of your individual and collective goals.

If you're single, focus on cultivating a strong sense of self-love, self-respect, and emotional resilience. Engage in activities that make you feel empowered, confident, and connected to your inner strength. Trust that by radiating your authentic light and energy, you will attract aligned and supportive connections into your life.

Career:

In your professional life, October 2025 invites you to align your work with your deepest values, passions, and purpose. With Mars moving through Libra and Scorpio this month, you may feel a strong drive to collaborate with others, take on leadership roles, and make a meaningful impact in your field or community.

However, with Mercury stationing retrograde in Scorpio on October 19th, you may need to review, revise, or reconsider certain projects, plans, or communication strategies in your work. Use this time to reassess your long-term goals, seek feedback from trusted mentors, and make any necessary adjustments to ensure that your career path is aligned with your authentic self and higher purpose.

Trust in the power of your intuition, creativity, and resilience to navigate any challenges or obstacles that arise. Remember that every setback is an opportunity for growth, learning, and self-discovery.

Finances:

In financial matters, October 2025 emphasizes the importance of deep transformation, shared resources, and aligning your investments with your values and long-term goals. The New Moon in Libra on October 21st is a powerful time to set intentions and create practical strategies for increasing your prosperity, abundance, and financial partnerships.

However, with Pluto stationing direct in Aquarius on October 13th, you may need to confront any fears, power struggles, or hidden dynamics related to money, debts, or joint financial ventures. Be willing to face the truth, take responsibility for your choices, and make any necessary changes to ensure that your financial foundation is built on integrity, transparency, and mutual trust.

Focus on cultivating a mindset of gratitude, generosity, and abundance, even in the face of challenges or limitations. Trust that by aligning your resources with your deepest values and purpose, you will attract the support and opportunities you need to thrive.

Health:

In matters of health and well-being, October 2025 invites you to embrace deep emotional healing, spiritual transformation, and holistic self-care. With the Sun, Mercury, and Venus moving through Scorpio this month, you may feel a strong desire to explore the mind-body-spirit connection, release old traumas or patterns, and connect with your inner power and resilience.

Pay attention to any physical symptoms, emotional triggers, or intuitive messages that may be guiding you towards areas of your life that need healing, release, or transformation. The Full Moon in Aries on October 6th is a powerful time for letting go of any self-defeating thoughts, behaviors, or habits that may be impacting your health and well-being.

Remember to prioritize rest, relaxation, and self-nurturing practices in your daily routines. Engage in activities that bring you a sense of peace, joy, and connection to your inner wisdom, such as meditation, yoga, or spending time in nature.

Travel:

In the realm of travel and adventure, October 2025 may bring opportunities for deep spiritual journeys, transformative retreats, or immersive experiences that challenge you to expand your mind, heart, and soul. With Mercury and Venus moving through Scorpio, you may feel a strong desire to explore the mysteries of life, death, and rebirth, and to connect with the hidden dimensions of reality.

If physical travel is not possible, consider embarking on inner journeys through practices like shadow work, shamanic journeying, or deep psychological exploration. Seek out teachers, workshops, or resources that inspire your curiosity and challenge you to grow beyond your comfort zone.

Trust in the transformative power of facing your fears, embracing change, and surrendering to the unknown. Remember that every journey, whether external or internal, is an opportunity for self-discovery, healing, and spiritual awakening.

Insights from the Stars:

The cosmic energies of October 2025 are inviting you to embrace your emotional depth, spiritual power, and transformative potential. With Saturn and Uranus forming harmonious aspects this month, you are supported in breaking free from old limitations, embracing innovative solutions, and building a stronger foundation for your dreams and aspirations.

Trust in the journey of your soul, even when the path seems dark, uncertain, or challenging. Know that your sensitivity, intuition, and compassion are your greatest strengths, guiding you towards your highest truth and purpose. Stay open to the signs, synchronicities, and miracles that surround you, and have faith in the unfolding of divine timing and grace.

Best Days of the Month:

October 6th: Full Moon in Aries - A powerful time for releasing self-limiting patterns, asserting your needs and desires, and reconnecting with your inner fire and passion.

October 13th: Pluto Direct in Aquarius - A supportive influence for transforming power dynamics, embracing social change, and aligning your actions with your highest ideals and vision.

October 21st: New Moon in Libra - A potent portal for setting intentions and planting seeds related to emotional healing, financial partnerships, and creating more balance and harmony in your life.

October 29th: Mercury enters Sagittarius - A helpful energy for expanding your mind, exploring new ideas and philosophies, and communicating your truth with optimism and faith.

October 30th: Mars enters Capricorn - A time for taking practical steps, setting realistic goals, and aligning your actions with your long-term aspirations and responsibilities.

November 2025

Overview Horoscope for the Month:

Dear Pisces, November 2025 is a month of spiritual exploration, emotional transformation, and personal growth. With the Sun in Scorpio illuminating your 9th house of higher learning, philosophy, and adventure until November 21st, you are called to expand your horizons, seek new experiences, and connect with your inner wisdom.

The New Moon in Scorpio on November 20th brings a powerful opportunity to set intentions and plant seeds related to your spiritual journey, long-distance travel, or educational pursuits. Trust your intuition and be open to unexpected opportunities for growth and self-discovery.

On November 21st, the Sun shifts into Sagittarius, activating your 10th house of career, public image, and long-term goals. This energy supports your professional aspirations and invites you to align your work with your values and vision for the future.

Love:

In matters of the heart, November 2025 emphasizes the importance of emotional depth, authenticity, and shared values in your relationships. With Venus moving through Scorpio and Sagittarius this month, you may find yourself attracted to partners who challenge you to grow, explore new ideas, and expand your understanding of love and intimacy.

If you're in a committed relationship, the Full Moon in Taurus on November 5th illuminates your 3rd house of communication and self-expression. Use this energy to have honest and heartfelt conversations with your partner about your needs, desires, and shared vision for the future. Be open to listening deeply and finding creative solutions to any challenges that arise.

If you're single, focus on cultivating a sense of adventure, curiosity, and openness in your social interactions. Engage in activities that align with your passions and values, and trust that your authentic self-expression will attract compatible and inspiring connections.

Career:

In your professional life, November 2025 invites you to take a visionary and proactive approach to your goals and aspirations. With Mars entering Sagittarius on November 4th, you may feel a strong drive to expand your skills, network, and opportunities for growth and success.

However, with Mercury stationing retrograde in Sagittarius on November 9th, you may need to review, revise, or reconsider certain projects, plans, or communication strategies in your work. Use this time to reassess your long-term objectives, gather feedback from trusted mentors, and make any necessary adjustments to align your career path with your higher purpose.

Trust in the power of positive thinking and optimism, even in the face of challenges or setbacks. Remember that your unique talents and perspective are valuable assets, and that every experience is an opportunity for learning and self-discovery.

Finances:

In financial matters, November 2025 emphasizes the importance of long-term planning, wise investments, and aligning your resources with your values and goals. With Jupiter and Neptune forming a supportive trine aspect mid-month, you may experience unexpected windfalls, opportunities for growth, or inspired ideas for increasing your prosperity and abundance.

However, with Mars in Sagittarius squaring Neptune, be mindful of any tendencies towards overspending, financial risk-taking, or unrealistic expectations. Stay grounded in your budgeting and decision-making, and seek the guidance of trusted advisors or professionals when needed.

Focus on cultivating a mindset of gratitude, generosity, and trust in the universe's ability to provide for your needs. Remember that true wealth involves a holistic balance of material, emotional, and spiritual well-being.

Health:

In matters of health and well-being, November 2025 invites you to expand your understanding of holistic healing, mind-body connection, and preventative care. With the Sun and Mercury moving through Scorpio and Sagittarius, you may feel drawn to explore new wellness practices, philosophies, or alternative therapies that support your physical, emotional, and spiritual health.

Pay attention to any areas of your life where you may be holding onto stress, tension, or unresolved emotions. The Full Moon in Taurus on November 5th is a powerful time for releasing old patterns, practicing self-care, and reconnecting with your body's natural rhythms and needs.

Remember to prioritize rest, relaxation, and joy in your daily routines. Engage in activities that bring you a sense of adventure, laughter, and connection to your inner child.

Travel:

In the realm of travel and adventure, November 2025 may bring opportunities for long-distance journeys, cultural immersions, or educational experiences that expand your mind and worldview. With the Sun and Mercury moving through Sagittarius, you may feel a strong desire to explore new horizons, connect with diverse communities, and broaden your understanding of the world.

If physical travel is not possible, consider embarking on inner journeys through practices like meditation, visualization, or shamanic journeying. Seek out teachers, workshops, or online resources that inspire your curiosity and feed your hunger for knowledge and personal growth.

Trust in the transformative power of new experiences and perspectives, even when they challenge your comfort zone or beliefs. Remember that every journey, whether external or internal, is an opportunity for self-discovery and soul evolution.

Insights from the Stars:

The cosmic energies of November 2025 are inviting you to embrace your spiritual wisdom, emotional depth, and visionary potential. With Saturn direct in your sign from November 27th onwards, you are supported in building a stronger foundation for your dreams and taking practical steps towards your long-term goals.

Trust in the journey of your soul, even when the path seems uncertain or challenging. Know that your sensitivity, compassion, and intuition are your greatest gifts, guiding you towards your highest purpose and destiny. Stay open to the signs, synchronicities, and miracles that surround you, and have faith in the unfolding of divine timing.

Best Days of the Month:
- November 5th: Full Moon in Taurus - A powerful time for releasing old patterns, practicing self-care, and reconnecting with your body's wisdom and needs.
- November 20th: New Moon in Scorpio - A potent portal for setting intentions and planting seeds related to your spiritual growth, higher education, and personal expansion.

- November 27th: Saturn Direct in Pisces - A supportive influence for taking practical steps, building a solid foundation, and aligning your actions with your soul's purpose.
- November 29th: Mercury Direct in Scorpio - A helpful energy for gaining clarity, integrating insights, and communicating your truth with depth and authenticity.
- November 30th: Venus enters Sagittarius - A time for expanding your heart, exploring new forms of love and connection, and aligning your relationships with your highest ideals and aspirations.

December 2025

Overview Horoscope for the Month:

Dear Pisces, December 2025 is a month of spiritual renewal, emotional healing, and personal growth. With the Sun in Sagittarius illuminating your 10th house of career, public image, and long-term goals until December 21st, you are called to align your professional path with your higher purpose, values, and vision for the future.

The New Moon in Sagittarius on December 19th brings a powerful opportunity to set intentions and plant seeds related to your career aspirations, leadership roles, and public contributions. Trust your intuition and be open to unexpected opportunities for growth, expansion, and success.

On December 21st, the Sun shifts into Capricorn, followed by the ingress of Mercury and Venus later in the month. This energy activates your 11th house of friendships, social networks, and community involvement, inviting you to connect with like-minded individuals, collaborate on shared goals, and make a positive impact in your social circles.

Love:

In matters of the heart, December 2025 emphasizes the importance of emotional maturity, commitment, and shared values in your relationships. With Venus moving through Sagittarius and Capricorn this month, you may find yourself attracted to partners who inspire you to grow, achieve your goals, and build a strong foundation for the future.

If you're in a committed relationship, the Full Moon in Gemini on December 4th illuminates your 4th house of home, family, and emotional roots. Use this energy to have honest conversations with your partner about your needs, desires, and long-term plans for your shared life together. Be open to finding creative solutions and compromises that honor both of your individual and collective aspirations.

If you're single, focus on cultivating a strong sense of self-awareness, emotional intelligence, and personal responsibility. Engage in activities that make you feel empowered, purposeful, and connected to your inner wisdom. Trust that by radiating your authentic light and energy, you will attract aligned and supportive connections into your life.

Career:

In your professional life, December 2025 invites you to take a visionary and strategic approach to your goals and aspirations. With the Sun, Mercury, and Venus moving through Sagittarius and Capricorn this month, you may feel a strong drive to expand your skills, take on leadership roles, and make a meaningful impact in your field or community.

However, with Mercury stationing retrograde in Capricorn on December 28th, you may need to review, revise, or reconsider certain projects, plans, or communication strategies in your work. Use this time to reassess your long-term objectives, seek feedback from trusted mentors, and make any necessary adjustments to ensure that your career path is aligned with your authentic self and higher purpose.

Trust in the power of your intuition, creativity, and resilience to navigate any challenges or obstacles that arise. Remember that every setback is an opportunity for growth, learning, and self-discovery.

Finances:

In financial matters, December 2025 emphasizes the importance of long-term planning, wise investments, and aligning your resources with your values and goals. With Saturn and Neptune forming harmonious aspects this month, you may experience a sense of clarity, inspiration, and divine guidance related to your financial situation and material aspirations.

Focus on creating a solid foundation for your future security and prosperity, while also being open to unexpected opportunities for growth and abundance. Trust in the universe's ability to provide for your needs and desires, and practice gratitude and generosity in your financial dealings.

Remember that true wealth involves a holistic balance of material, emotional, and spiritual well-being, and that your inner state of abundance and contentment is the key to attracting outer prosperity and success.

Health:

In matters of health and well-being, December 2025 invites you to embrace a holistic and proactive approach to your physical, emotional, and spiritual well-being. With the Sun, Mercury, and Venus moving through Sagittarius and Capricorn this month, you may feel a strong desire to establish healthy routines, take responsibility for your choices, and align your lifestyle with your long-term goals and aspirations.

Pay attention to any areas of your life where you may be experiencing stress, imbalance, or neglect, and take practical steps to address these issues with compassion and self-care. The Full Moon in Gemini on December 4th is a powerful time for releasing mental clutter, communicating your needs and boundaries, and finding a healthy balance between work and rest.

Remember to prioritize activities that bring you joy, relaxation, and a sense of connection to your inner wisdom and divine purpose. Engage in practices like yoga, meditation, or spending time in nature to nourish your mind, body, and soul.

Travel:

In the realm of travel and adventure, December 2025 may bring opportunities for long-distance journeys, cultural exchanges, or experiences that expand your mind, broaden your horizons, and align with your spiritual path and purpose. With Jupiter forming harmonious aspects this month, you may feel a strong desire to explore new ideas, philosophies, and ways of being in the world.

If physical travel is not possible, consider embarking on inner journeys through practices like visualization, dreamwork, or studying the wisdom traditions of different cultures. Seek out teachers, workshops, or resources that inspire your curiosity and challenge you to grow beyond your comfort zone.

Trust in the transformative power of new experiences and perspectives, even when they challenge your assumptions or beliefs. Remember that every journey, whether external or internal, is an opportunity for self-discovery, learning, and spiritual evolution.

Insights from the Stars:

The cosmic energies of December 2025 are inviting you to embrace your spiritual wisdom, emotional maturity, and creative potential. With Saturn and Neptune forming harmonious aspects this month, you are supported in manifesting your dreams, aligning your actions with your higher purpose, and trusting in the divine plan for your life.

Stay open to the signs, synchronicities, and miracles that surround you, and have faith in the unfolding of divine timing and grace. Know that your sensitivity, compassion, and intuition are your greatest gifts, guiding you towards your highest truth and destiny.

Remember that you are a divine being of love and light, with a unique purpose and path to unfold in this lifetime. Trust in the wisdom of your soul, the guidance of your heart, and the support of the universe as you navigate the transformative energies of December 2025.

Best Days of the Month:

- December 4th: Full Moon in Gemini - A powerful time for releasing mental clutter, communicating your truth, and finding a healthy balance between work and rest.

- December 10th: Neptune Direct in Pisces - A supportive influence for spiritual awakening, creative inspiration, and aligning your actions with your highest ideals and vision.

- December 19th: New Moon in Sagittarius - A potent portal for setting intentions and planting seeds related to your career aspirations, leadership roles, and public contributions.

- December 26th: Sun conjunct Jupiter in Capricorn - A time for expanding your vision, embracing new opportunities, and aligning your actions with your long-term goals and aspirations.

- December 29th: Mercury stations retrograde in Capricorn - A helpful energy for reviewing, revising, and refining your plans, communication strategies, and long-term objectives.

57431719R00065